# Mandala Coloring Book for Adults

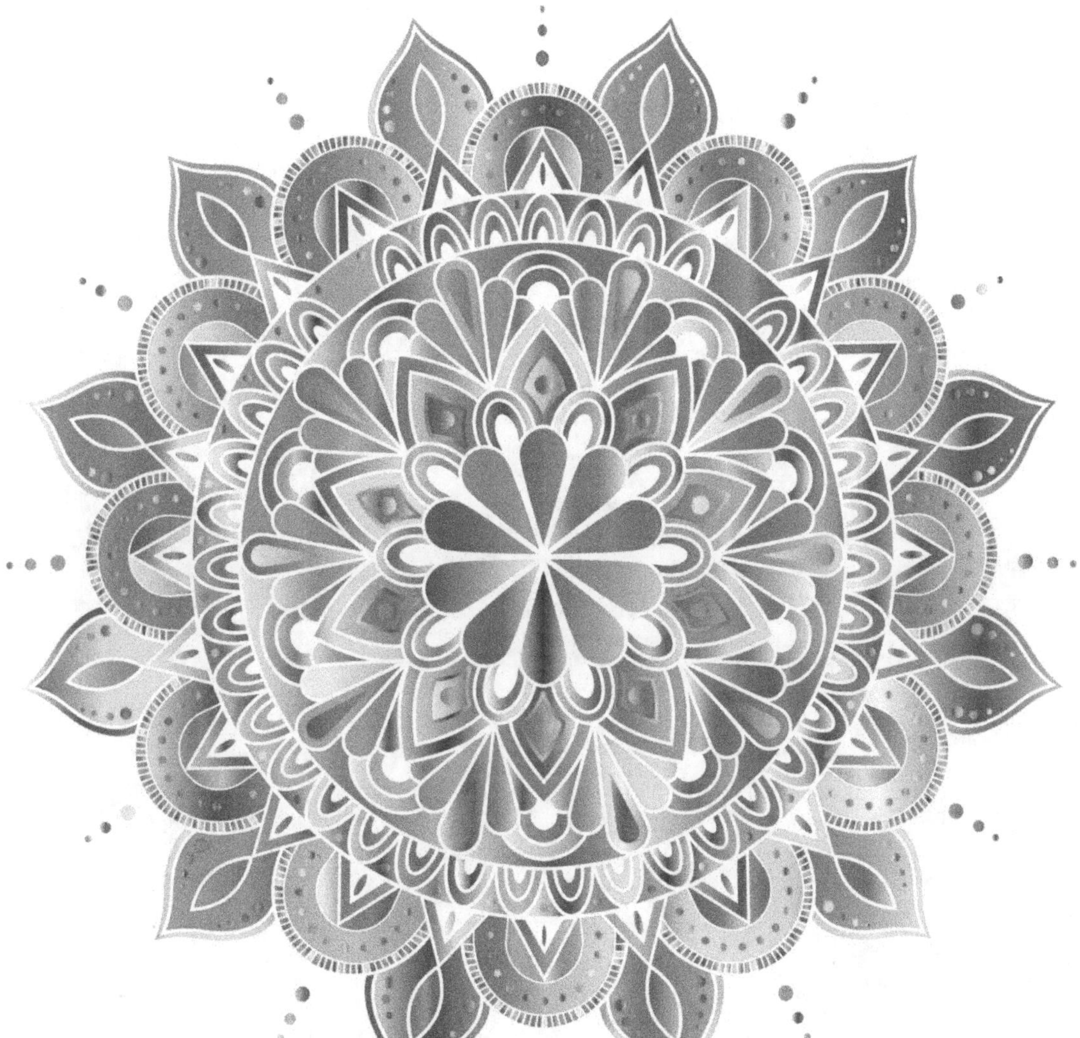

This Book Bélongs To :

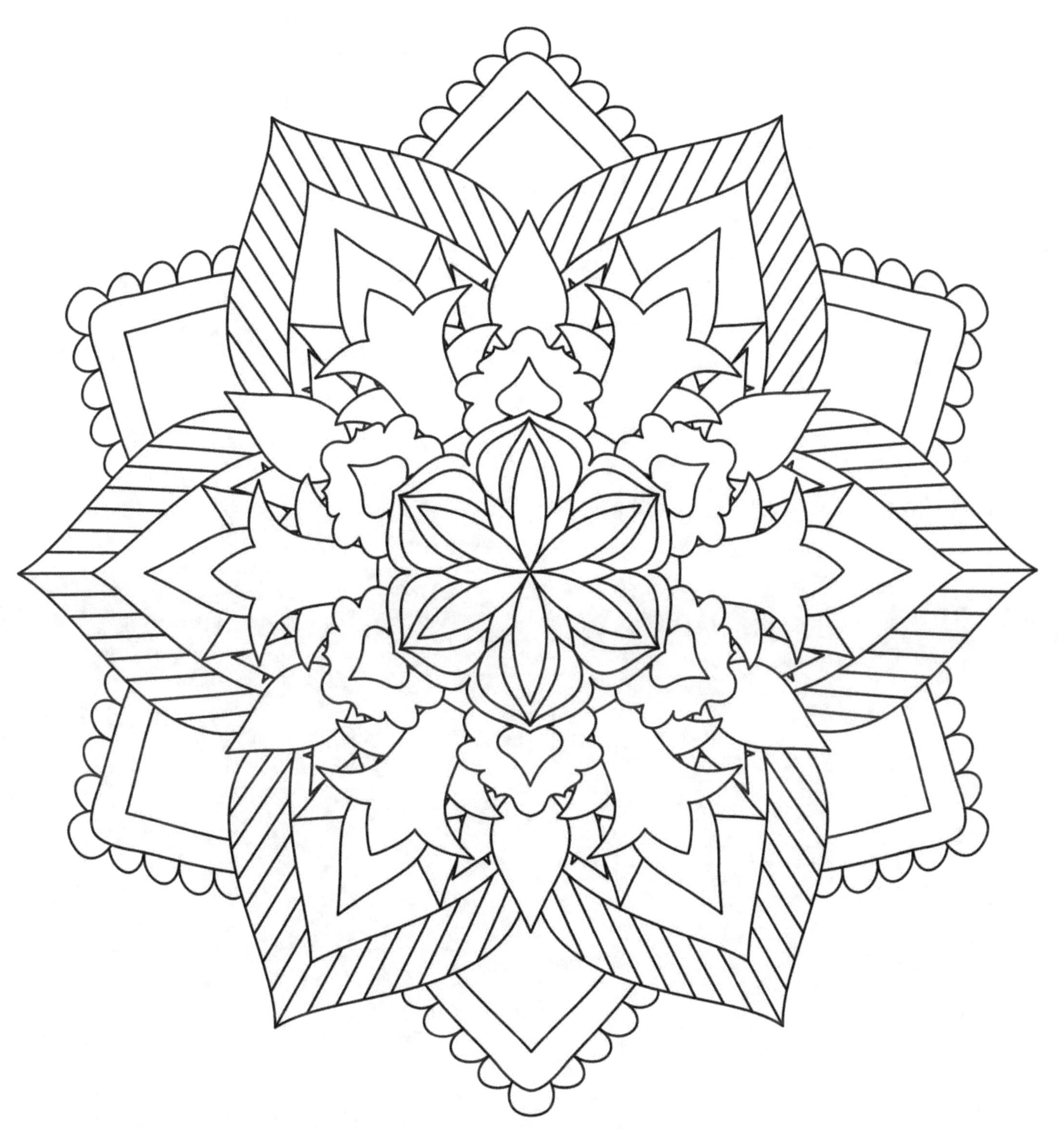

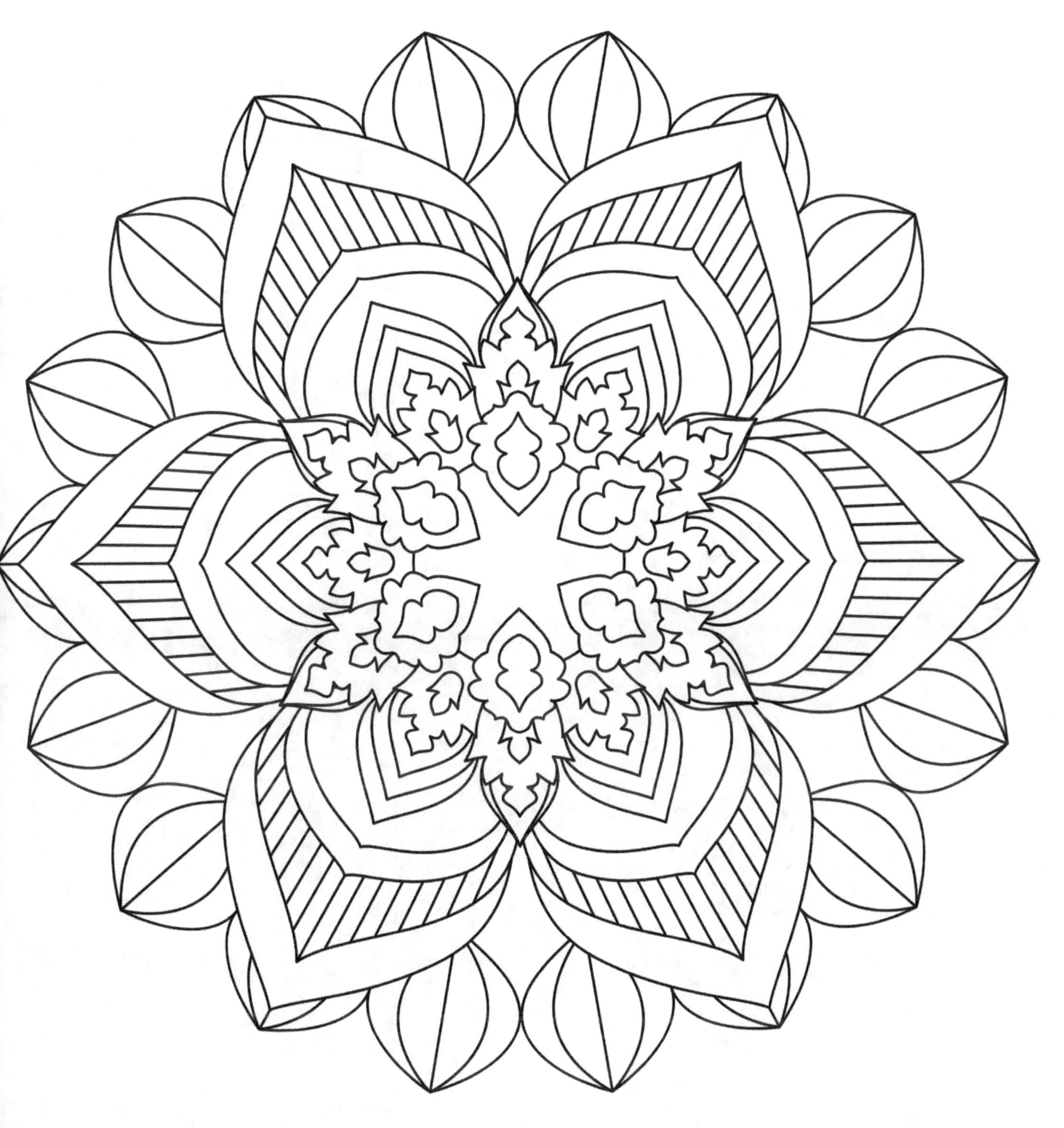

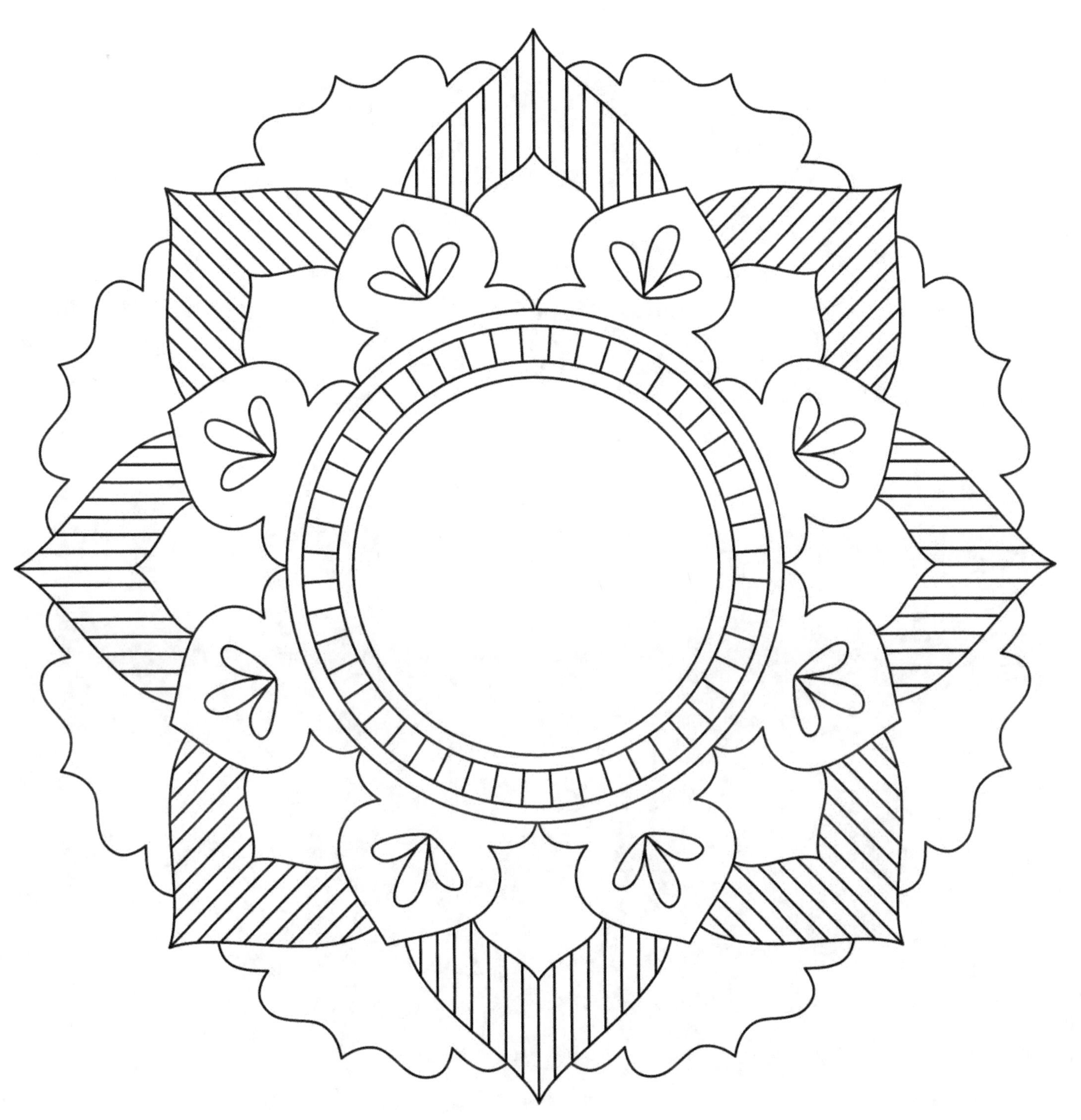

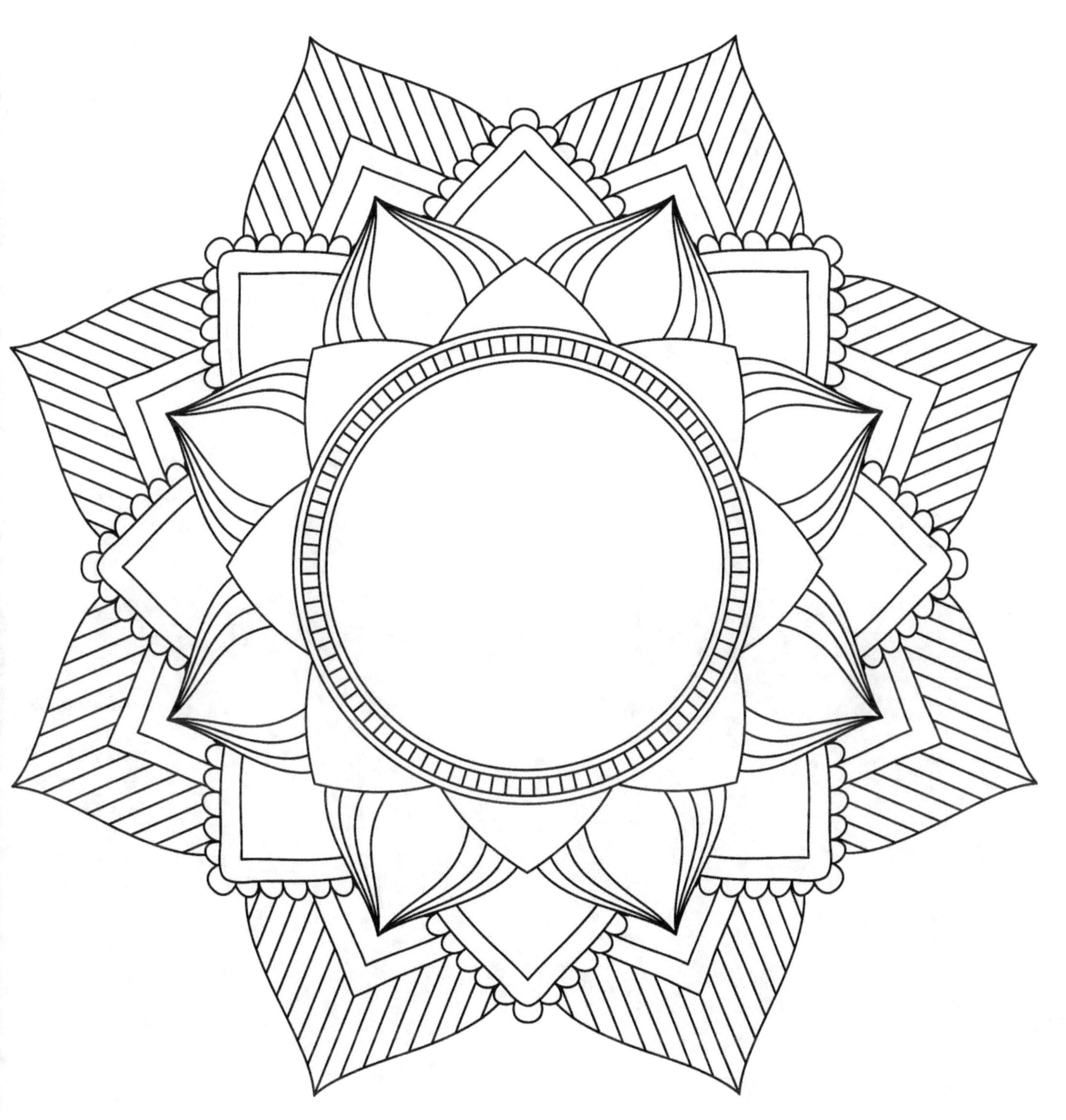

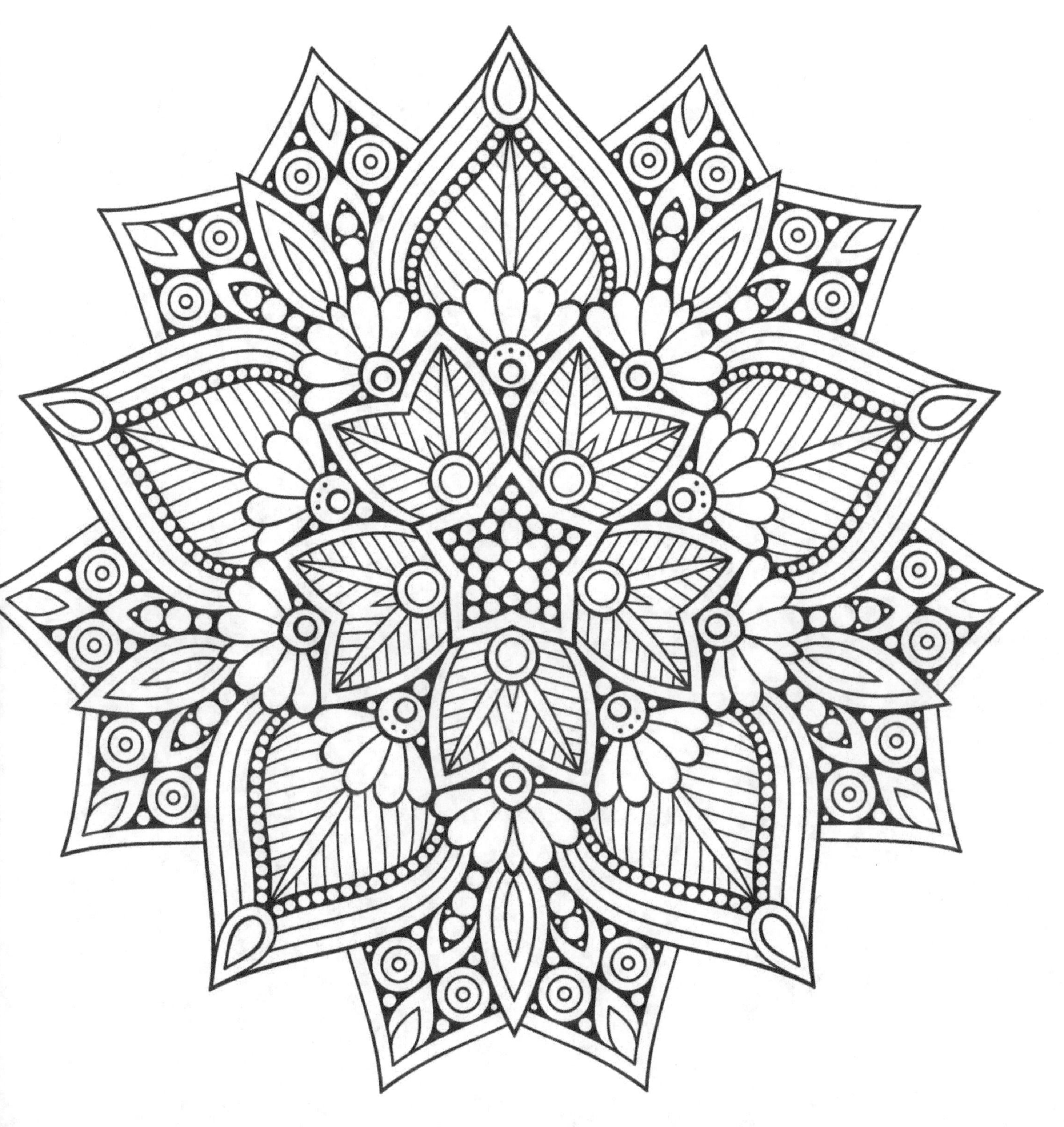

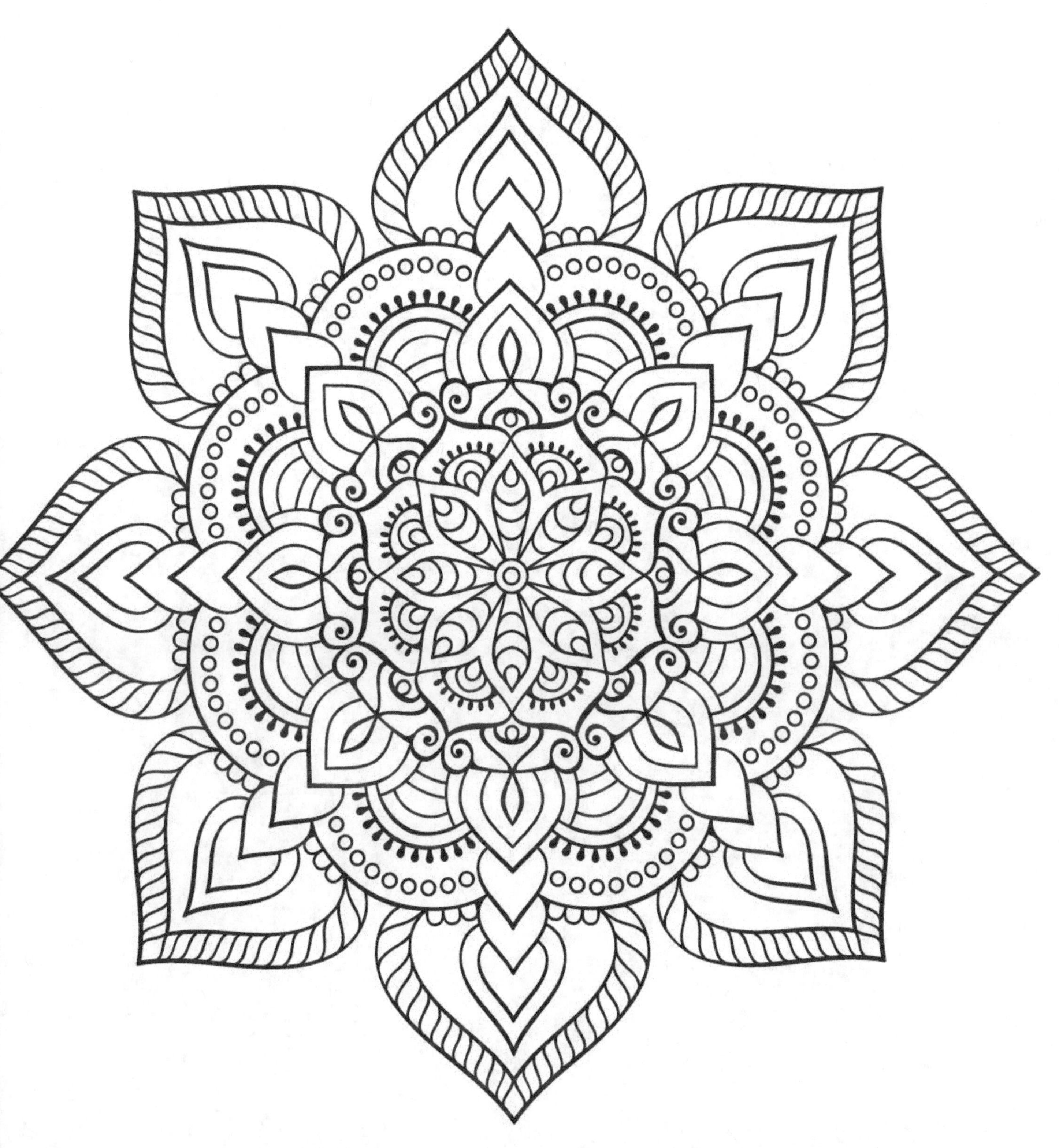

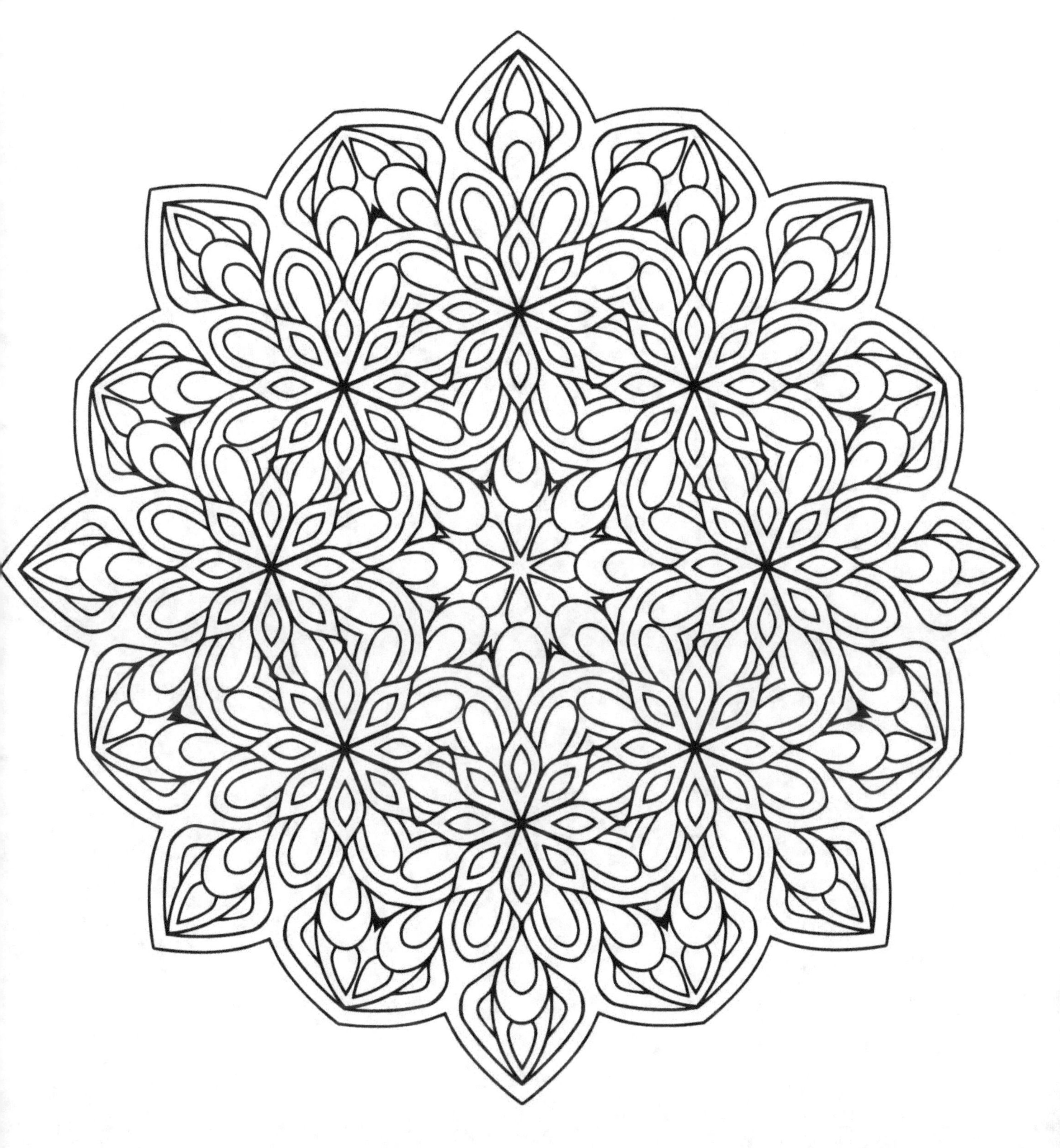

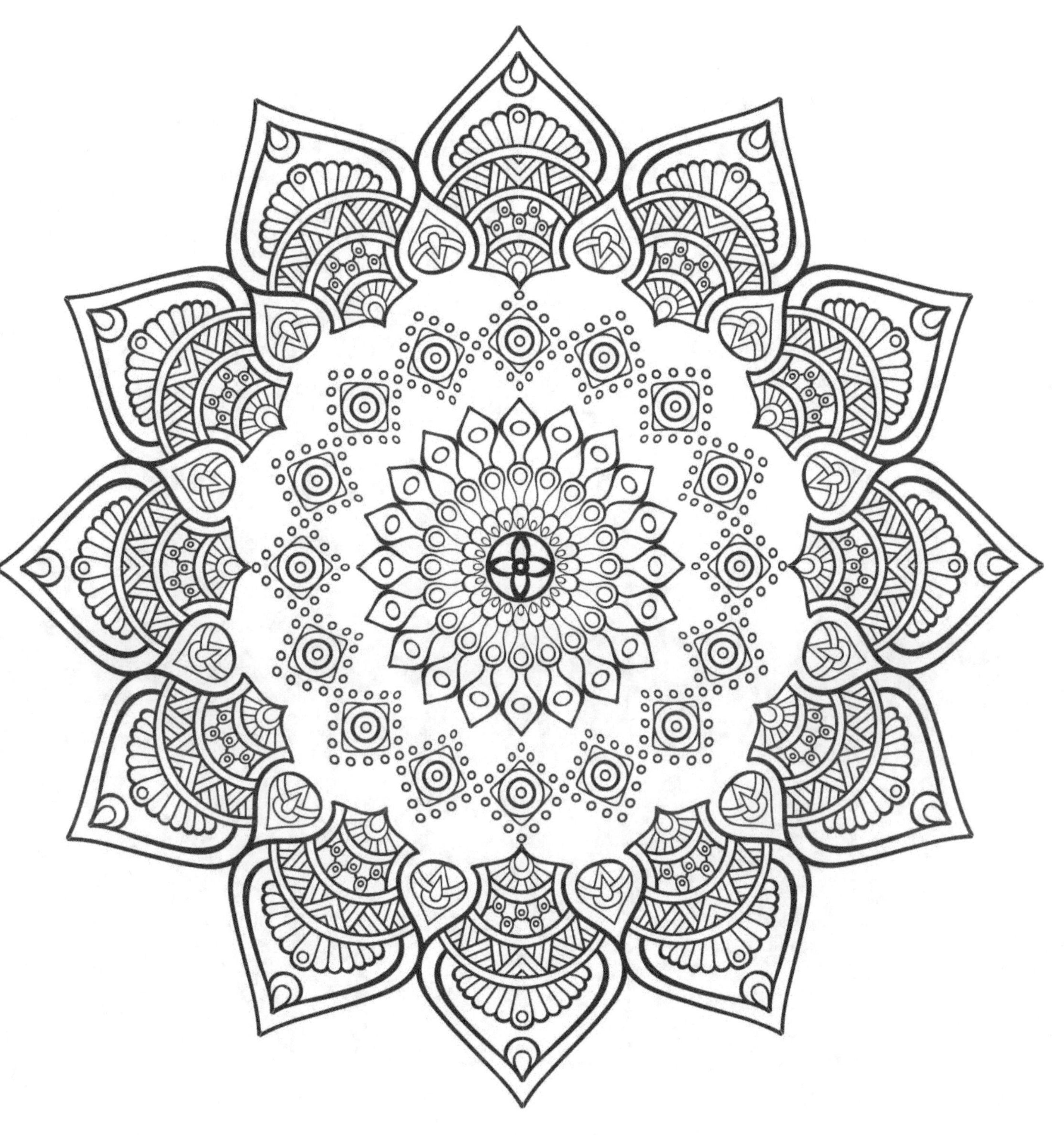

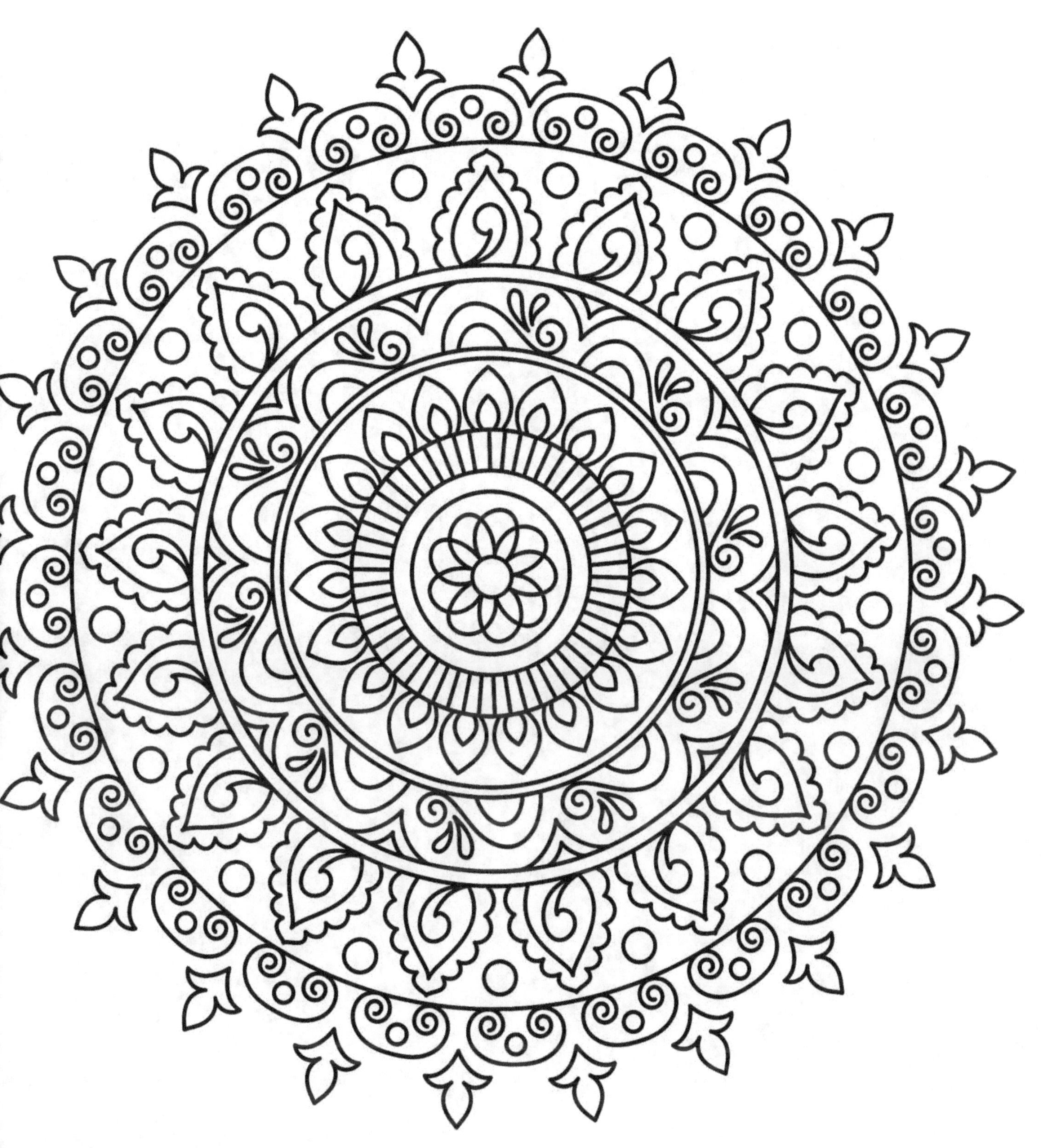

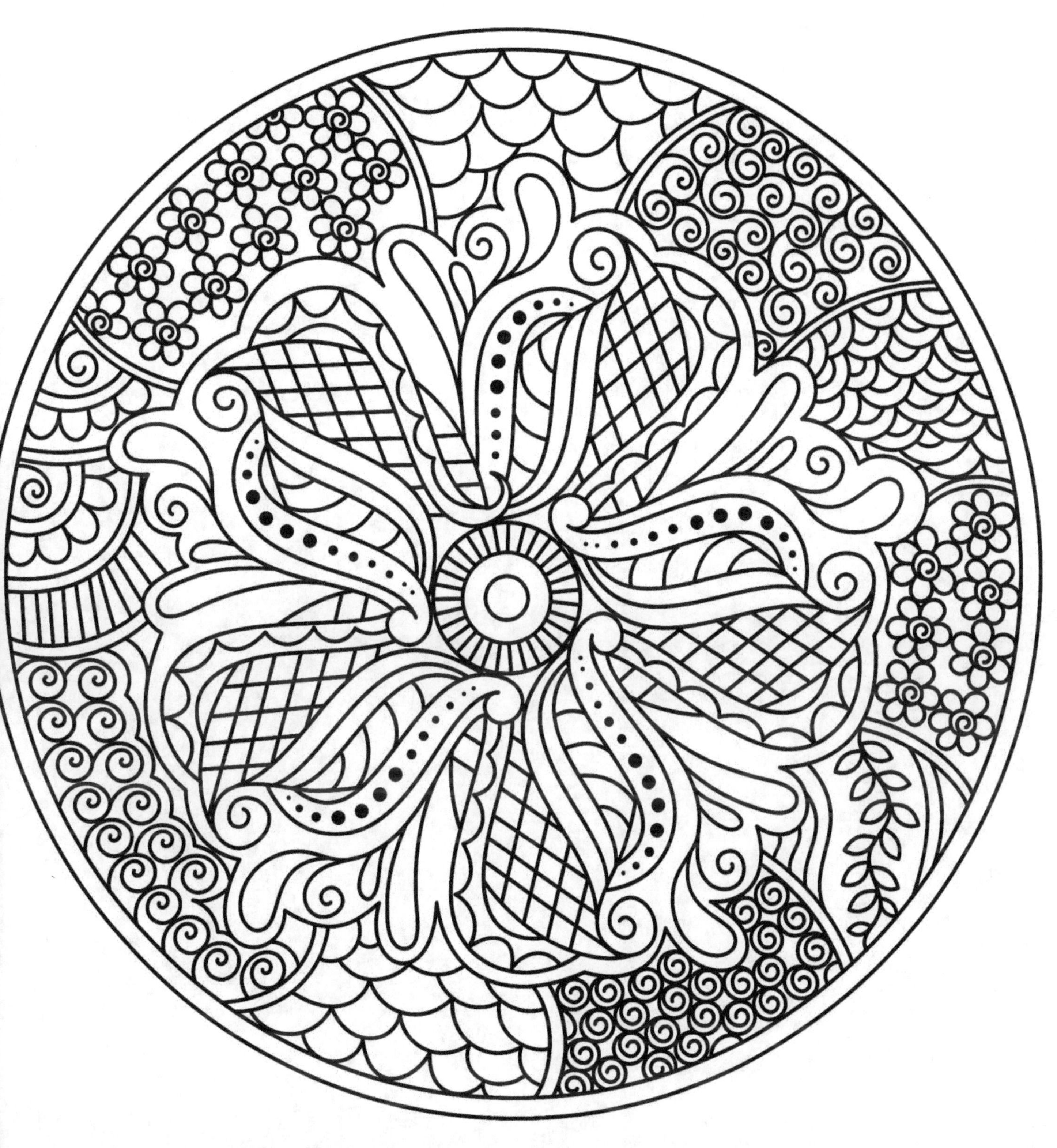

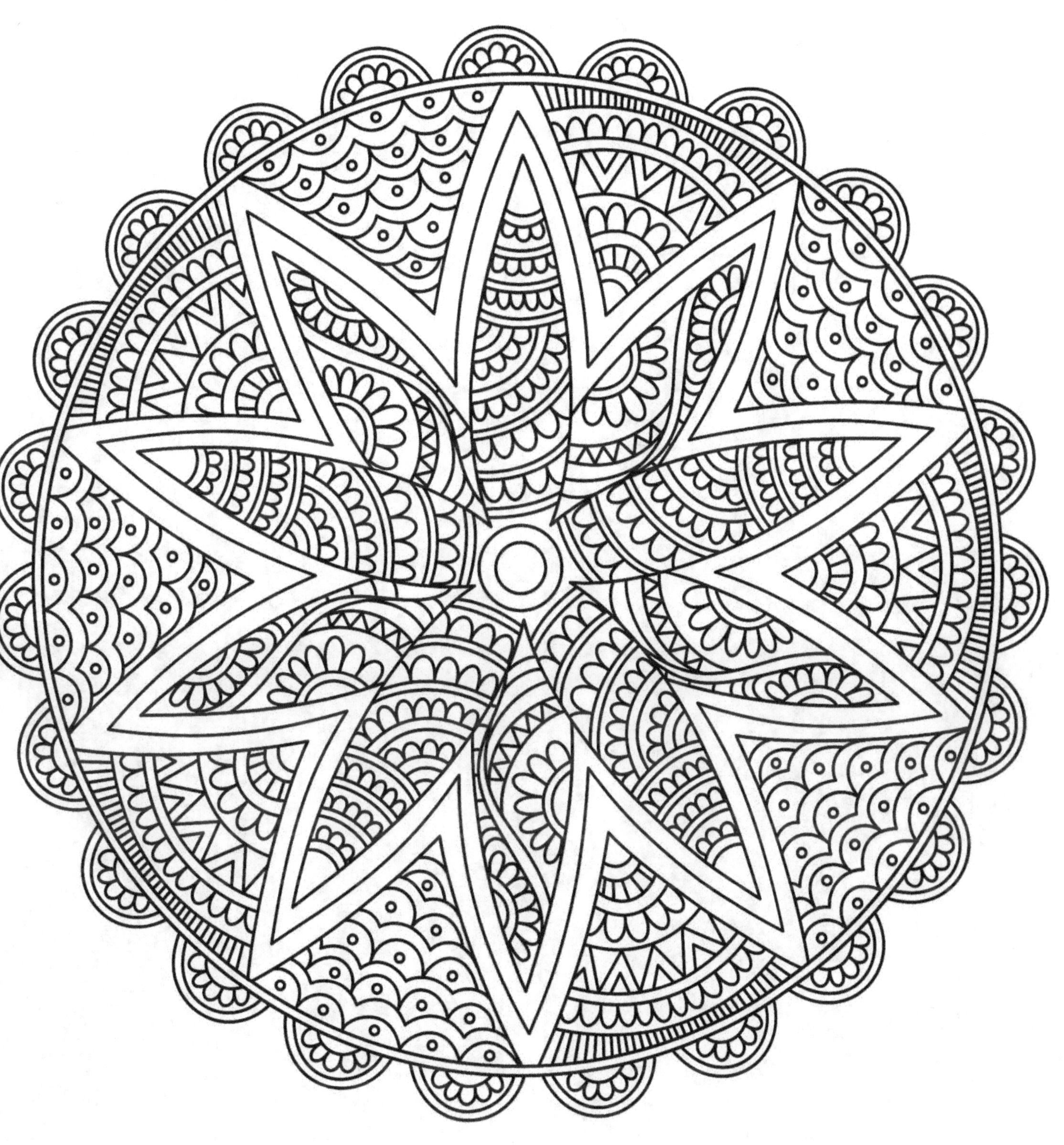

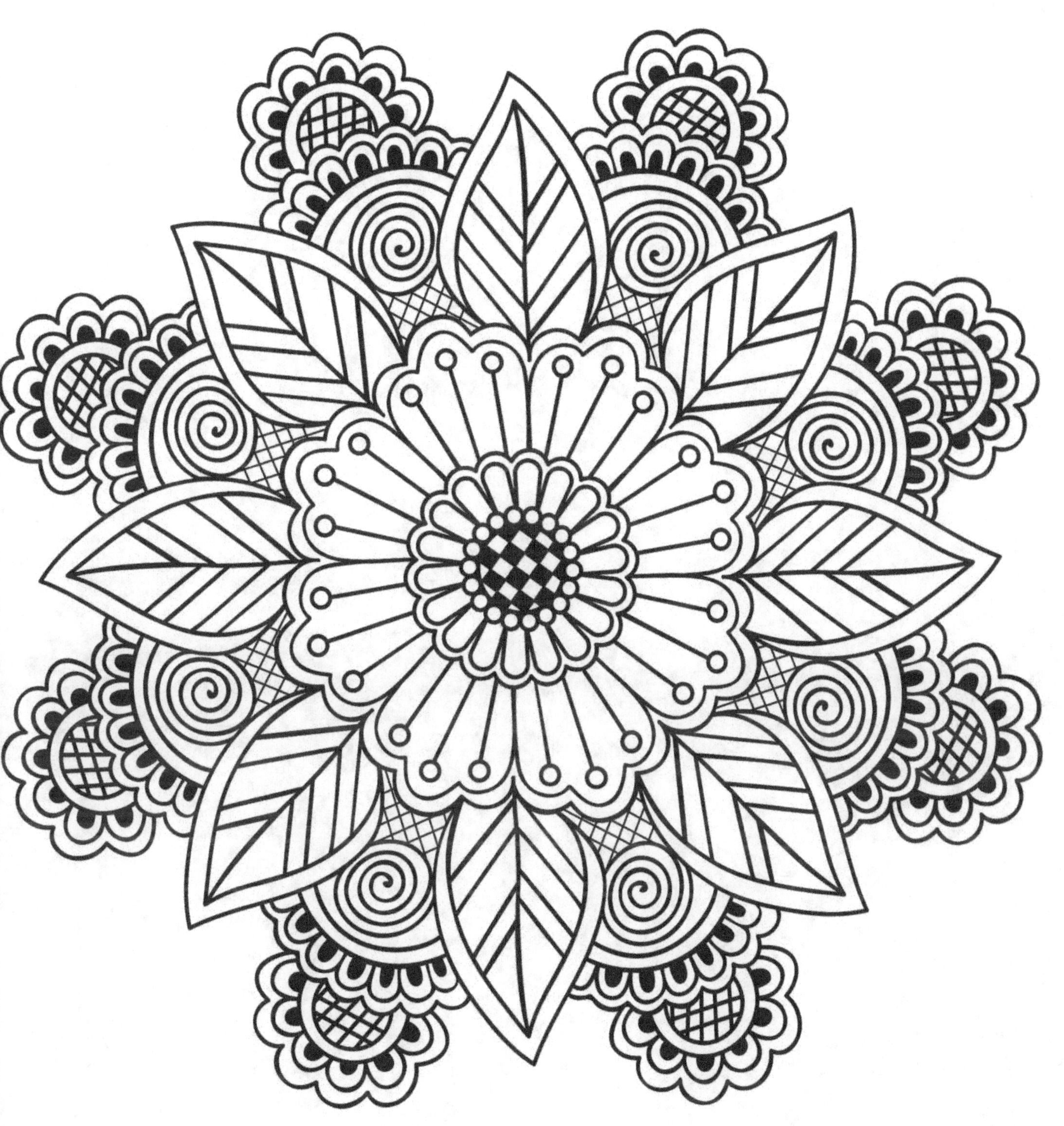

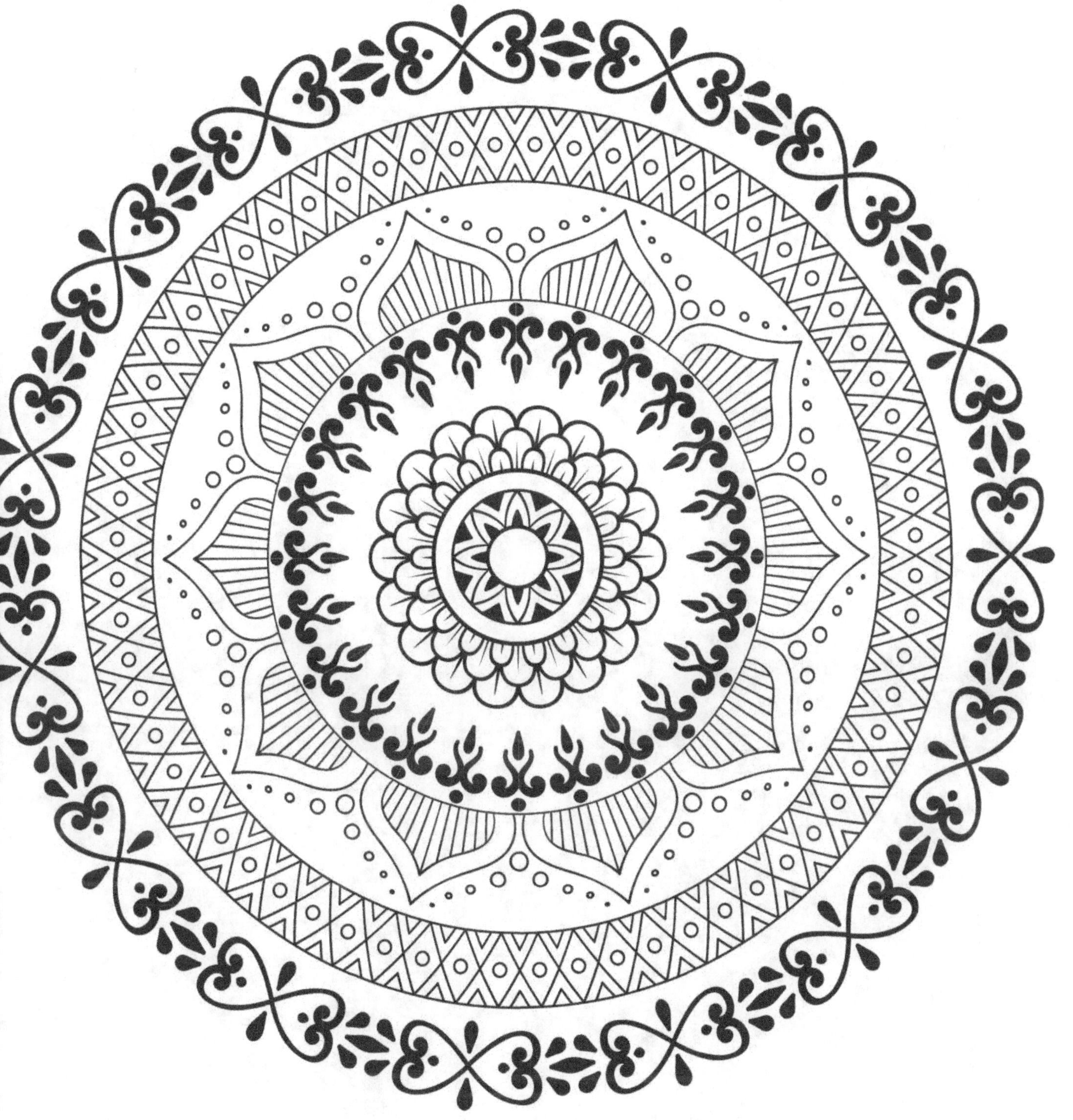

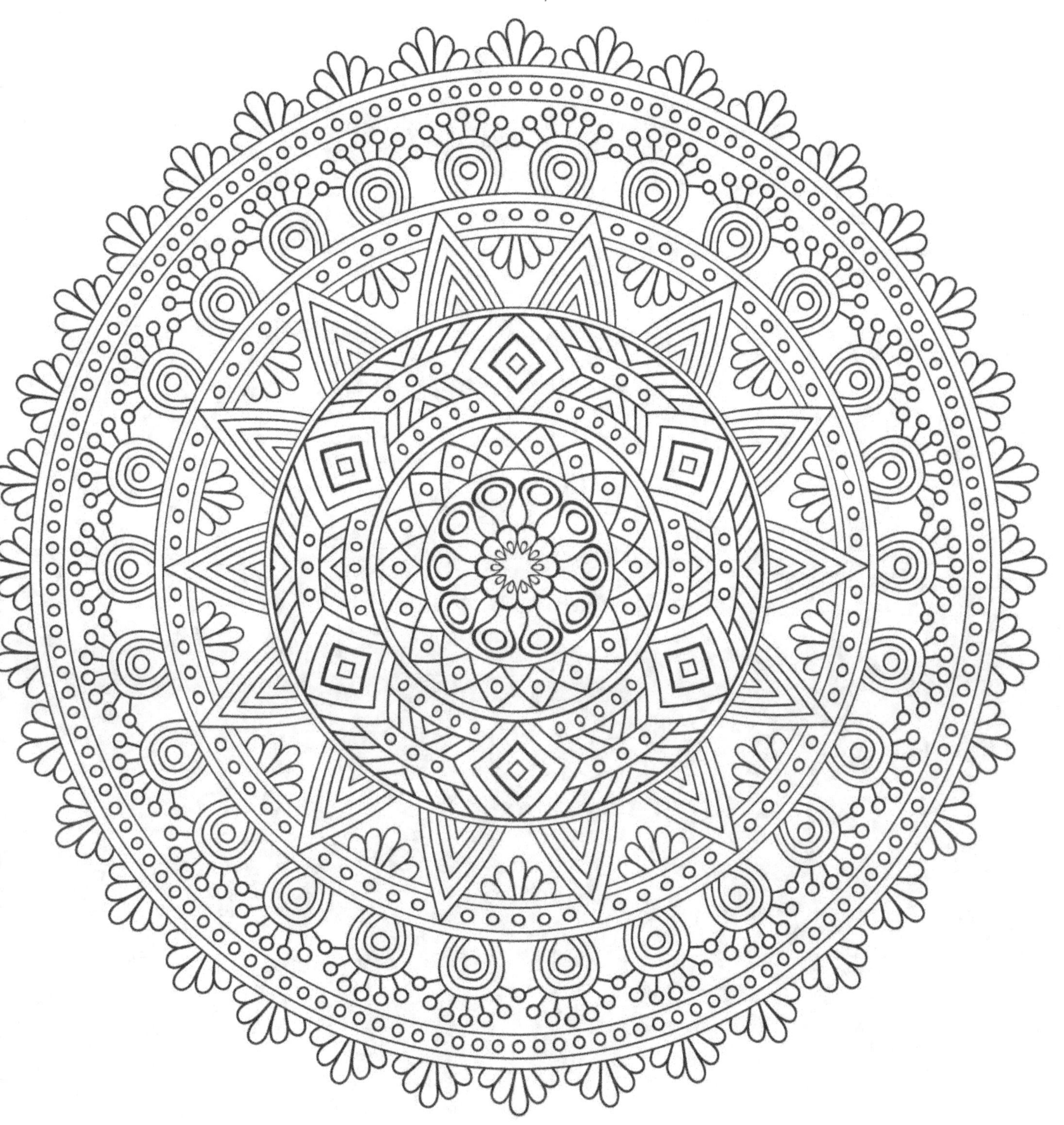

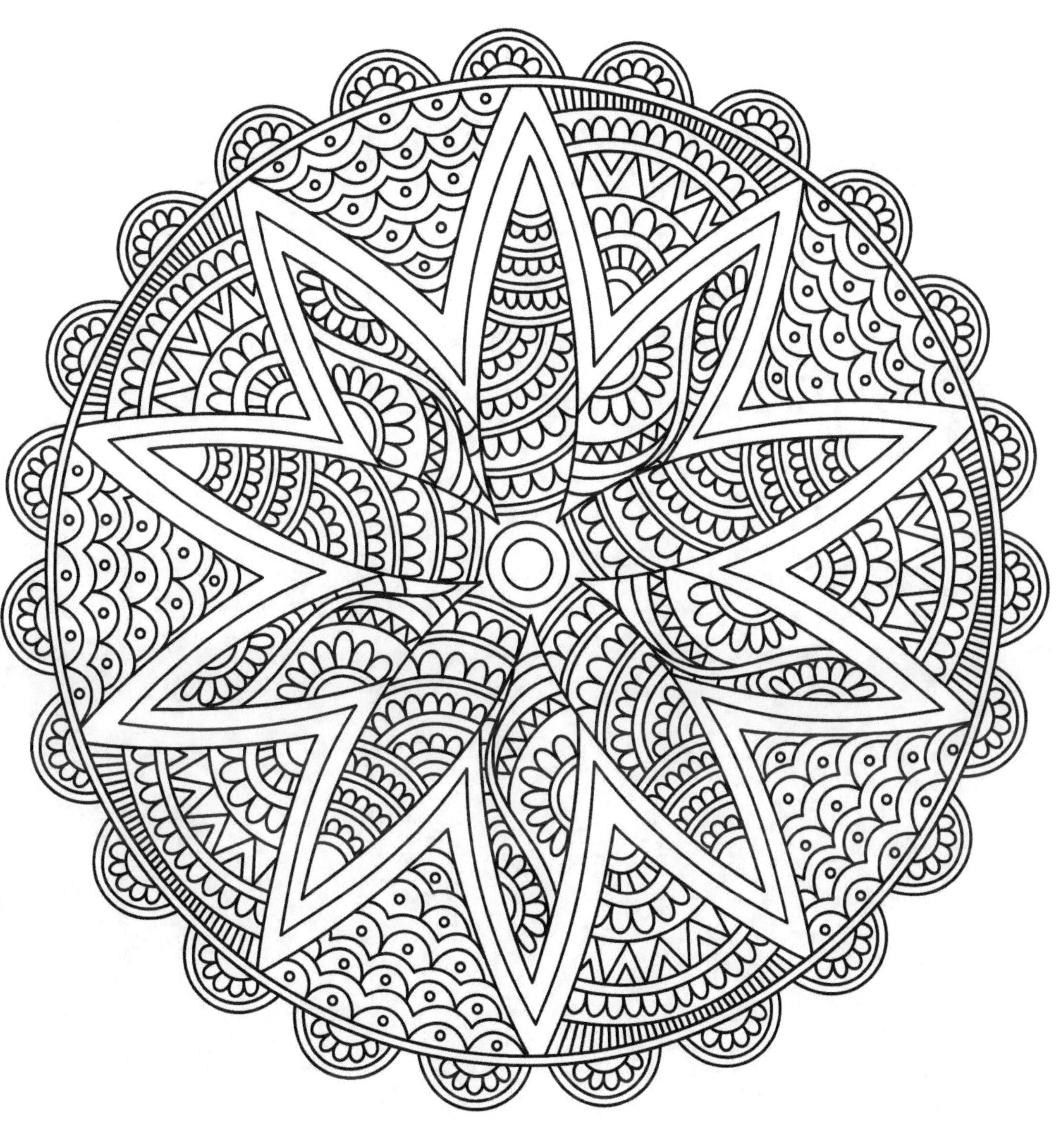

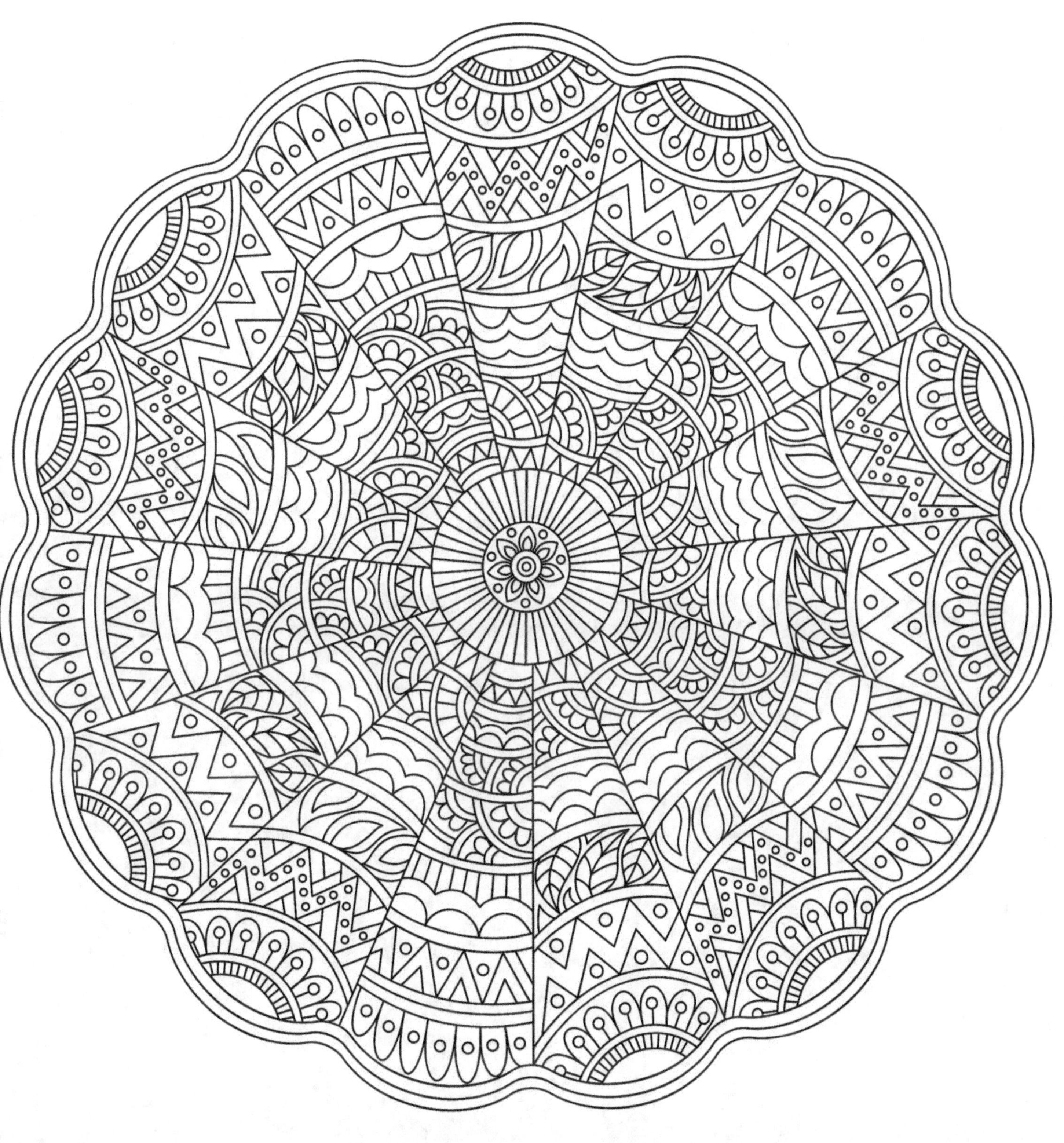

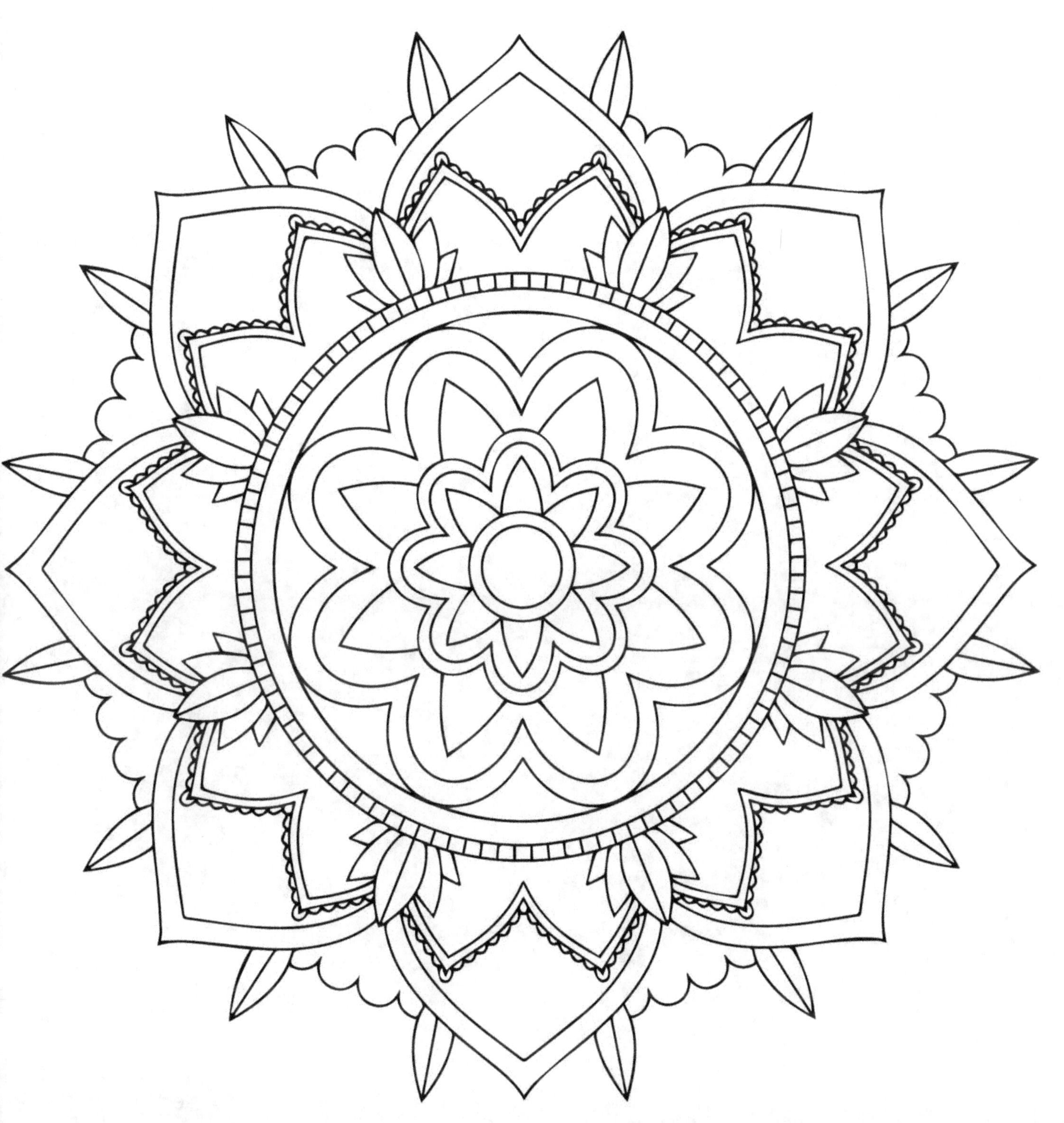

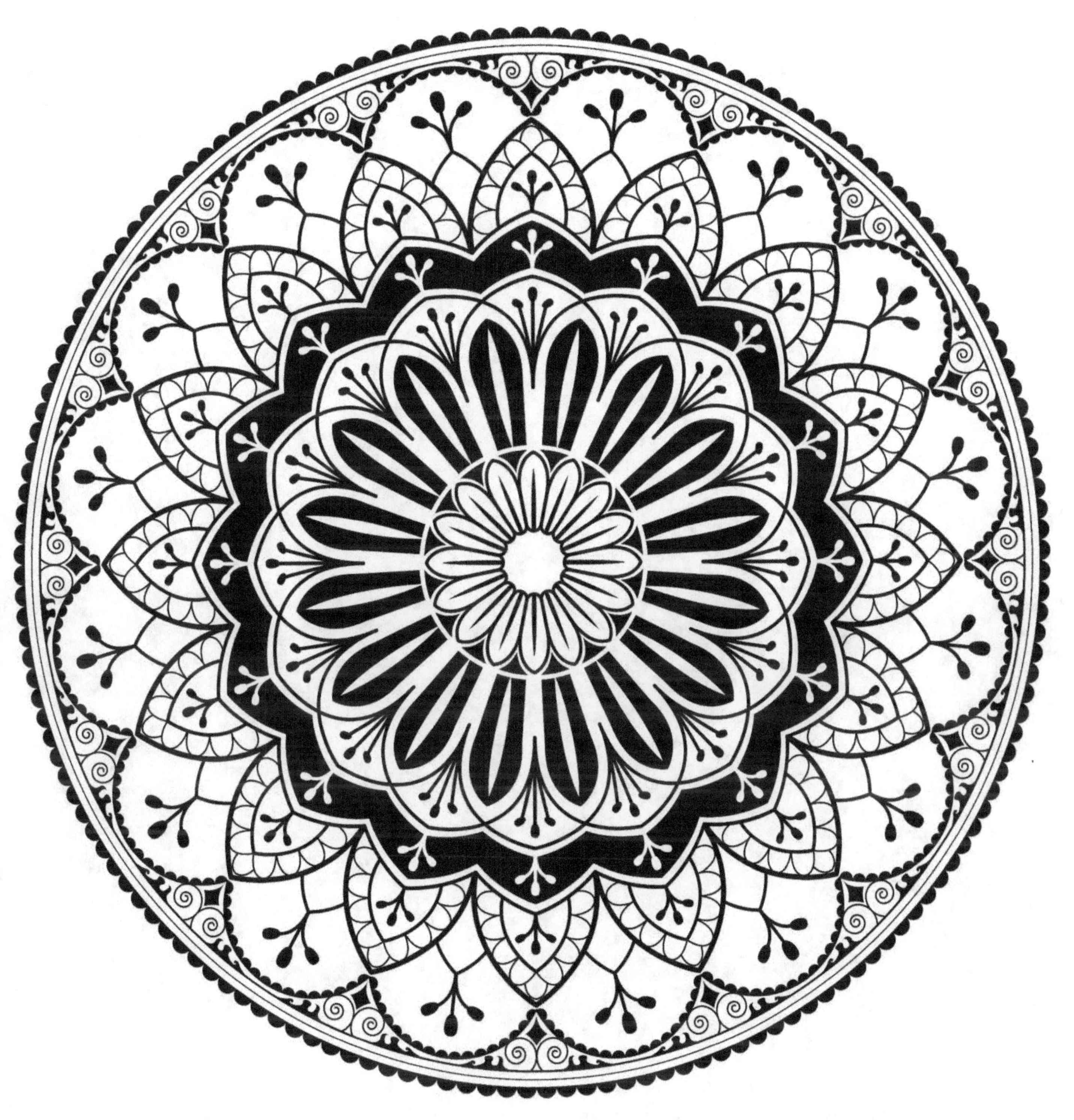

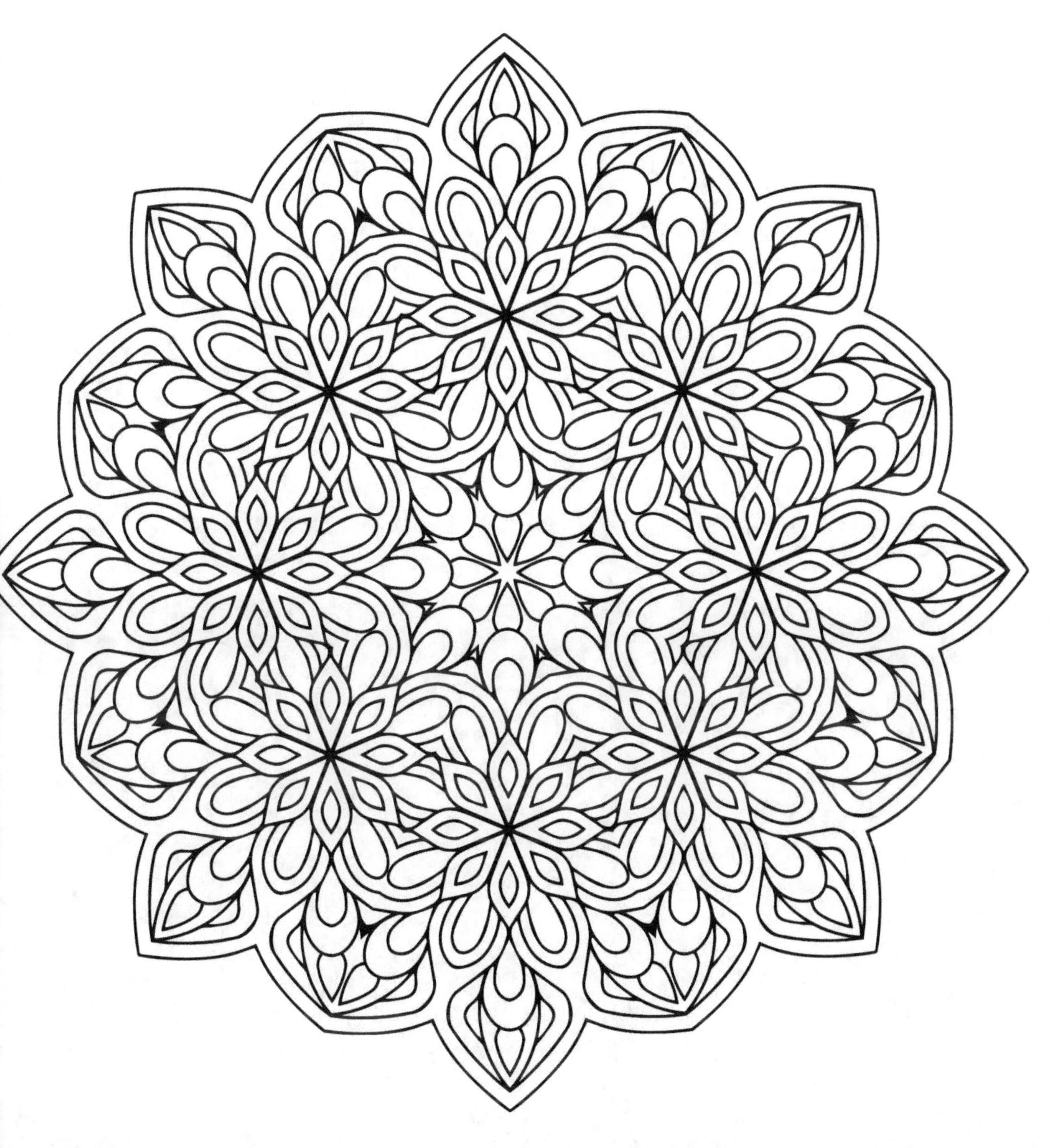

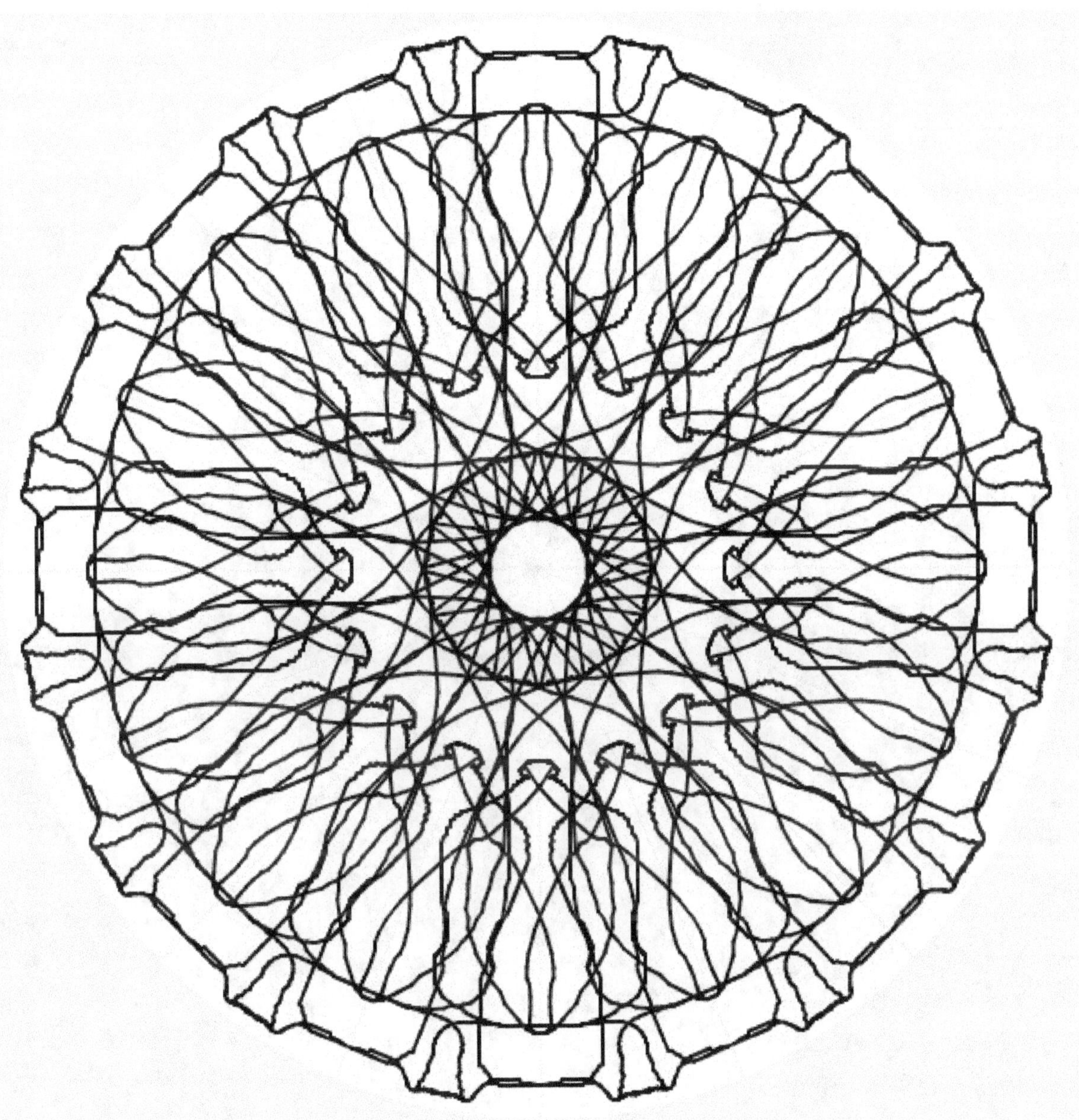

# Thank You For Buying My Book

www.ingramcontent.com/pod-product-compliance
Lightning Source LLC
Chambersburg PA
CBHW081309250726
48662CB00008B/2476